Charity
Key to Gospel
Motivation

Charity
Key to Gospel Motivation

by

Merlin O. Baker

ISBN: 1-55517-466-3
v.1

Published by Bonneville Books

Distributed by:
925 North Main, Springville, UT 84663 • 801/489-4084

CFI Publishing and Distribution Since 1986
Cedar Fort, Incorporated
CFI Distribution • CFI Books • Council Press • Bonneville Books

Typeset by Virginia Reeder
Cover design by Adam Ford
Cover design © 2000 by Lyle Mortimer

Printed in the United States of America

CONTENTS

ACKNOWLEDGMENT

I acknowledge a great debt to the Lord for a call to serve as president of a mission of his Church, for the revelation to strive by precept and example to love the missionaries and members of the Canada Halifax Mission and for their great example of dedication and love for me and my family – for these spiritual experiences were the genesis of the thoughts expressed in this book.

CHARITY

A mother's gentle touch across her
newborn's face,
A hand that lifts when hope is gone,
Silence when injustice cries from within,
Unanswered prayers renewed each day by
faith.

Forgiveness without judgment or
remembrance,
Tears for the proud who slip and fall,
Unconditional, unfettered love,
Peace within, though storms rage without.

My crimson sins washed white as snow,
That night alone – Gethsemane,
A silent voice within, arise, rejoice,
My love and blood hath made you clean and
free.

Merlin O. Baker

CHAPTER ONE

INTRODUCTION

People do not lack strength
they lack will.

Victor Hugo

Strength, knowledge, ability or talent do not assure success in the endeavors of this life nor in the development of spirituality. Desire, will and motivation bring success and accomplishment. Look about you and observe those who are spiritual giants. Be assured that they have developed their spiritual talents and abilities through the exercise of their agency—they apparently were motivated by some great force to achieve their spiritual attainments. Why are some spiritually motivated and others are not? Why do many who have great spiritual knowledge and even profess a testimony, fail to act upon it or act only hesitantly or sporadically? Why is the gift of eternal life which is so freely offered so often not accepted?

For what doth it profit a man if a gift is bestowed upon him, and he recieves not the gift?

Behold, he rejoices not in that which is given unto him, neither rejoices in him who is the giver of the gift. [D&C 88:33]

Behold, here is the agency of man, and here is the condemnation of man; because that which was from the beginning is plainly manifest unto them, and they receive not the light.[D&C 93:31]

Why are the glories and blessings of eternity disregarded with so little thought in favor of the illusory and transitory pleasures of the world? Why are so many satisfied with such trifles as the wealth, power and acclaim of men when the infinite power and glory of God are within their grasp?

Logic would compel the conclusion that anyone who knows the gospel principles—that we are the literal children of God, and that by obedience we can gain ultimate happiness and become as God— would bend every effort to act upon such knowledge. But such is not the case. Gospel knowledge and testimony do not guarantee action, even when that action would be in the best self-interest of an individual.

Some might contend that those who do not act on their spiritual knowledge really do not "know". This may be true in some instances, but observation and personal experience indicate that in most cases it is not so. Or perhaps we can question that the knowledge they have is more of the head than of the heart. "They know in their minds but their hearts have not been activated; their spirits have not been stirred with heavenly power". [Lynn A. McKinlay, *The Spirit Giveth Life*, (Salt Lake City: Deseret News Press, 1955) 12]

To truly know a gospel principle, it must not only be understood, but must be experienced. To know the divine power and love of God, they must be experienced.

Why so many individuals seemingly act so illogically and against their own self-interest is beyond the scope of this book. The burden of this book is to try to discover the key to gospel motivation—that which will motivate individuals to make the logical and right choices to insure their eternal happiness.

As a necessary foundation, certain fundamental gospel principles such as our eternal right to choose and our ultimate potential and destiny are first examined. Different levels of gospel motivation—fear, duty and reward, and charity, or the pure love of Christ, are discussed. The conclusion is reached that the most powerful gospel motivational force is the pure love of Christ. Without it we are at great risk that our will and desire will not be strong enough to secure the goal and blessing of exaltation. The book concludes by suggesting how the gift of charity, this tremendous gospel motivational force, can be acquired in our lives.

It is the prayerful desire of the author that those who may read and ponder the message of this book will come to experience, perhaps for the first time, or more deeply, the sweetness and power of charity, the pure love of Christ and that it will become the driving force of their gospel obedience and service.

CHAPTER TWO

FREE AGENCY: OUR POWER TO GAIN OR LOSE EXALTATION

The Prophet Joseph Smith taught that we have always had our free agency. Intelligence, that uncreated individual part of each of us, which makes us co-eternal with God, had as an essential attribute the right to choose:

> *The intelligence of spirits had no beginning, neither will it have an end. That is good logic. That which has a beginning may have an end.... Intelligence is eternal and exists upon a self-existent principle... there is no creation about it.* [Joseph Fielding Smith, *Teachings of the Prophet Joseph Smith,* (Salt Lake City: Deseret News Press, 3d ed. 1942), 353-54]

> *Man was also in the beginning with God. Intelligence, or the light of truth, was not created or made, neither indeed can be.*
>
> *All truth is independent in that sphere in*

> *which God has placed it, to act for itself, as all intelligence also; otherwise there is no existence.*[D&C 93:29-30]

The scriptures do not reveal how this attribute of free agency was manifest prior to the incorporation of our intelligence into our spirit body. However, as spirit children of our Eternal Father, we exercised our free agency at the Grand Council in heaven. Two plans for our future development were placed before us: the plan of our Eternal Father, championed by Jesus Christ, and the plan of Lucifer, Son of the Morning. Heavenly Father's plan was based on free agency, the right and opportunity to choose between good and evil, and a Redeemer to redeem us from the consequences of our sins upon condition of repentance. The plan of Lucifer, required the negation of the eternal principle of free agency.

We considered the two opposing plans. The Savior advocated Heavenly Father's plan and Lucifer spoke for his plan. We exercised our free agency and chose to follow the plan of our Eternal Father. However, one-third of the assembled spirits rejected the plan of their spiritual Father and chose to follow the plan of their spirit brother, Lucifer:

> *"A third part of the hosts of heaven turned he away from me because of their agency." [D&C 29:36]*

Because of their choice, this one-third of Heavenly Father's spirit children were denied the privilege to have a physical body. They will be cast into outer darkness, to suffer the torment of a damned soul for all eternity. No one can conceive of the suffering of those who chose to follow Lucifer—only those who made such a decision or those on this earth who, through the exercise of their free agency, become Sons of Perdition.

> *And the end thereof, neither the place thereof, nor their torment, no man knows;*
>
> *Neither was it revealed, neither is, neither will be revealed unto man, except to them who are made partakers thereof;*
>
> *Nevertheless, I, the Lord, show it by vision unto many, but straightway shut it up again;*
>
> *Wherefore, the end, the width, the height, the depth, and the misery thereof, they understand not, neither any man except those who are ordained unto this condemnation. [D&C 76:45-48]*

To even try to imagine the terrible punishment that those who chose to follow Lucifer have and will suffer eternally is to begin to comprehend the awesome power of free agency and the eternal consequences which follow its exercise. We each possess this great power, but take it so much for granted and exercise it so casually.

We are here in mortality because in our first estate we exercised our agency and followed Heavenly Father's plan. What will be our choice here in mortality? How we exercise our free agency will determine our future eternal possibilities. We are still free to choose.

> *Wherefore, men are free according to the flesh; and all things are given them which are expedient unto man. And they are free to choose liberty and eternal life, through the great Mediator of all men, or to choose captivity and death, according to the captivity and power of the devil; for he seeketh that all men might be miserable like unto himself. [2 Nephi 2:27]*

The exercise of our free agency in the pre-existence had eternal consequences, as will its exercise here in mortality. To contrast the glory and power of the celestial kingdom with that of the telestial kingdom, is to gain a further understanding of the power of free agency:

> *They who dwell in his presence are the church of the Firstborn; and they see as they are seen, and know as they are known, having received of his fulness and of his grace.*
>
> *And he makes them equal in power, and in might, and in dominion.*
>
> *And the glory of the celestial is one, even as the glory of the sun is one.*
>
> *And the glory of the terrestrial is one, even as the glory of the moon is one.*

> *And the glory of the telestial is one, even as the glory of the stars is one; for as one star differs from another star in glory, even so differs one from another in glory in the telestial world; [D&C 76:94-98]*

A moment's serious reflection in contrasting the brightness of the sun at noonday with a twinkling star at midnight should indelibly burn into our souls the awesome power of individual free agency and the eternal consequences of its exercise.

Although we have our free agency—the right to choose—once a choice is made, consequences follow as a result of inexorable eternal law. God administers the gospel plan in accordance with eternal law. He is no respecter of persons. He plays no favorites. As we sow, so shall we reap. As we obey divine law, we reap the promised blessing. When we are disobedient and do not repent, we reap condemnation and damnation. Yet God does not condemn us; we condemn ourselves through the exercise of our own free agency.

After Lucifer and those that followed him in the spirit world made their choice, the consequence of that decision became irreversible. There will never be an opportunity for those spirits to reverse their decision made in the pre-existence.

Mortality is a probationary state. Wrong decisions, with few exceptions, can be reversed, the consequences erased, and the sin forgiven. The atonement of Jesus Christ makes this possible as we are willing to repent and change our lives.

However, there will come a time when our probationary state will be over, and the day of repentance past, when the decisions we have made will become irreversible; the die will be cast, never to be changed:

> *For behold, this life is the time for men to prepare to meet God; yea, behold the day of this life is the day for men to perform their labors.*
>
> *And now, as I said unto you before, as ye have had so many witnesses, therefore, I beseech of you that ye do not procrastinate the day of your repentance until the end; for after this day of life, which is given us to prepare for eternity, behold, if we do not improve our time while in this life, then cometh the night of darkness wherein there can be no labor performed.*
>
> *Ye cannot say, when ye are brought to that awful crisis, that I will repent, that I will return to my God. Nay, ye cannot say this; for that same spirit which doth possess your bodies at the time that ye go out of this life, that same spirit will have power to possess your body in that eternal world.*
>
> *For behold, if ye have procrastinated the day of your repentance even until death, behold, ye have become subjected to the spirit of the devil, and he doth seal you his; therefore, the Spirit of the Lord hath withdrawn from you, and hath no place in you, and the devil hath all power over you; and this is the final state of the wicked. [Alma 34:32-35]*

After this mortal probation the day of repentance

will be past. Jeremiah spoke of this discomforting truth when he prophesied to wayward Israel: "The harvest is past, the summer is ended and we are not saved." [Jer. 8:20]

The phrase "eternal progression", which is familiar to members of the Church, is misleading unless the word "eternal" is equated with God. The word "eternal" is one of the names of God.

> *Behold, I am God; Man of Holiness is my name; Man of Counsel is my name; and Endless and Eternal is my name, also. [Moses 7:35]*

Just as "eternal punishment" does not mean punishment forever, but God's punishment [D&C 19:6-12], "eternal progression" is the progression that God offers each of us through the gospel plan. The phrase "eternal progression" does not mean that one will be able to continue to progress eternally (forever) in a quest to become like God irrespective of choices made in mortality. Such is not the case. The exercise of our free agency in mortality will determine for all eternity whether we will be as God. After the end of our mortal probation[1] there will be no second chance.

The Savior taught this truth plainly when he spoke of those who will inherit the telestial kingdom, those who will be as innumerable as the stars in the heavens:

1. This includes the period in the spirit world before the resurrection for those who had no opportunity to receive the gospel in mortality. [D&C 137,138]

> *For they [telestial kingdom] shall be judged according to their works, and every man shall receive according to his own works, his own dominion, in the mansions which are prepared;*
>
> *And they shall be servants of the Most High; but where God and Christ dwell they cannot come, worlds without end. [D&C 76:111-112]*

President Spencer W. Kimball has said:

> *After a person has been assigned to his place in the kingdom, either the telestial, the terrestrial or the celestial, or to his exaltation, he will never advance from his assigned glory to another glory. That is eternal! That is why we must make our decisions early in life and why it is imperative that such decisions be right.* [Spencer W. Kimball, *The Miracle of Forgiveness,* (Salt Lake City: Bookcraft, 1969), 243-244]

Our mortal probation in its time dimension is infinitesimal when compared with the duration of eternity. It is but a fleeting moment. However, the significance and consequence of our mortal probation is incalculable. So much is determined by the choices which we make in these few years called mortality.

One of the greatest tools that Satan has to defeat the exaltation of the children of God is to convince them that their decisions in mortality will always be reversible, that they will always be given a "second chance" even after their mortal probation is over.

> *And there shall also be many which shall say: Eat, drink, and be merry; nevertheless, fear God—he will justify in committing a little sin; yea, lie a little, take the advantage of one because of his words, dig a pit for thy neighbor; there is no harm in this; and do all these things, for tomorrow we die; and if it so be that we are guilty, God will beat us with a few stripes, and at last we shall be saved in the kingdom of God. [2 Nephi 28:8]*
>
> *And thus we see, that there was a time granted unto man to repent, yea a probationary time, a time to repent and serve God.*
>
> *Therefore, according to justice, the plan of redemption could not be brought about, only on conditions of repentance of men in this probationary state, yea, this preparatory state; for except it were for these conditions, mercy could not take effect except it should destroy the work of justice. Now the work of justice could not be destroyed; if so, God would cease to be God.* [Alma 42:4,13]

We have many "second chances" during our mortal probation. Each time the Holy Ghost prompts us to change the direction of our lives, we are given a second chance. Each time a living prophet speaks to our heart, we are given a second chance. It is critical that these changes be made in this life. Every one will be given an opportunity to accept or reject the gospel. However, those who reject the gospel during this life and then accept it later in the spirit world, will inherit the terrestrial kingdom, not the celestial kingdom. [D&C 76:76] Those who are not valiant in their testimony of Jesus Christ will also inherit the terrestrial kingdom [D&C 76:79]. The doctrine of the unlimited second chance is not of God but of him who would defeat our exaltation.

Elder Bruce R. McConkie taught:

> *There is no such thing as a second chance to gain salvation. This life is the time and the day of our probation. After this day of life, which is given us to prepare for eternity, then cometh the night of darkness wherein there can be no labor performed.*

***

> *Those who reject the gospel in this life and then receive it in the spirit world go, not to the celestial, but to the terrestrial kingdom.* [Bruce R. McConkie, "The Seven Deadly Heresies", *1980 BYU Speeches of the Year, 12-13*]

We are and will ultimately become what we have chosen. Also, there are critical "hinge points", in God's eternal plan, when the effect of choices remain throughout all eternity. What we choose and become in mortality forever limits our future choices and opportunities. To believe otherwise is to indulge in the greatest rationalization and the cruelest self-deception.

Free agency is a great blessing. It is the essence of life and existence; and as such, it is an awesome power. The power, through the gift of the Savior's atonement, to celestialize our spirit and body and to become like God, or, on the other hand, to become eternally less than our God-given potential.

We should be seriously concerned about the choices we make in this life. The Savior is concerned and without violating our agency does everything possible to help us make the right decisions. He is trying to motivate us to keep all of His commandments so that we can become as He is and and dwell with Him eternally. But God will not and cannot infringe upon our sacred right of free agency. There are bounds set by eternal law over which He cannot cross.

In subsequent chapters we will discuss what means the Savior uses to motivate us to obey the commandments. We will discover how to acquire the key to gospel motivation. Having acquired the key to gospel motivation, we will then have acquired the key to our own exaltation.

CHAPTER THREE

ETERNAL LIFE: KNOWLEDGE, TESTIMONY OR BECOMING LIKE THE SAVIOR?

The greatest gift of God is eternal life. [D&C 14:7] Eternal life is not synonymous with immortality, for everyone will exist through all eternity. Eternal life is God's life, to have and enjoy the quality of life that our Heavenly Father and Jesus Christ enjoy, to be perfect as They are perfect—to have the same knowledge, power, glory, dominion, as They have. [Bruce R. McConkie, "Making Our Calling and Election Sure", *1969 BYU Speeches of the Year, 5*]

> *They who dwell in his presence are the church of the Firstborn; and they see as they are seen, and know as they are known, having received of his fulness and of his grace;*
>
> *And he makes them equal in power, and in might, and in dominion. [D&C 76:94,95]*

The path to eternal life starts with the acquisition

of knowledge: the knowledge of God and our relationship to Him, the requirements of the eternal gospel plan, and the Savior's role in making the gospel plan effective in our lives. As we gain this knowledge, start obeying the commandments, and humble ourselves in prayer, we can gain a spiritual witness, a testimony, that the gospel plan is real and true. Through individual revelation from the Holy Ghost, we gain a knowledge of the truth of the gospel.

But a knowledge and testimony of the gospel or of the divinity of Jesus Christ alone will not secure for us the gift of eternal life. There are many examples of those who have understood the gospel and had testimonies, but who will not achieve celestial glory. Lucifer, a Son of the Morning, and those who followed him know that Jesus is the Christ, yet they fight unceasingly against Him. The evil spirits cast out by Jesus during his earthly ministry testified: "What have we to do with thee, Jesus, thou Son of God? Art thou come hither to torment us before the time?" [Matt. 8:29] "And unclean spirits, when they saw him, fell down before him, and cried, saying, Thou art the Son of God." [Mark 3:11]

The Apostle James declared to the early saints:

> *Thou believest that there is one God; thou doest well: the devils also believe, and tremble. [James 2:19]*

Many members of the Church will inherit the terrestrial and not the celestial kingdom because they were not "valiant" in their testimony. [D&C 76:79] President Spencer W. Kimball, in commenting on this scripture, has said that many Church members will not receive their promised blessings because of their unwillingness to do the will of their Heavenly Father, keep the commandments, and serve with all their might, mind, and strength in building the kingdom of God. [Spencer W. Kimball, *The Miracle of Forgiveness* (Salt Lake City: Bookcraft, 1969), 315]

Knowing the gospel is true is a necessary foundation, but the real purpose of mortality is in doing the will of God and becoming like the Savior.

> *And we will prove them herewith, to see if they will do all things whatsoever the Lord their God shall command them. [Abr. 3:25]*

> *Therefore, what manner of men ought ye to be? Verily I say unto you, even as I am. [3 Nephi 27:27]*

To gain eternal life, "to know the only wise and true God and Jesus Christ, whom he hath sent" [D&C 132:24] means more than knowing about God or having a testimony.

As stated by Arthur R. Bassett:

> *I believe that Christ, when he speaks of knowing him, is referring to the third sense of the word—not just that we know of him by reading about him or by hearing about him, but that we know him through the bonds of common experience and common feeling....*
>
> *If he becomes a central influence in our lives, I think we will come to seek his way of*

> *life just as we seek the course of life pointed out to us by the actions and thoughts of our earthly friends. We will begin to see things as though through his eyes, and sense things more deeply, as though through the depths of his feelings. As we begin to find ourselves becoming more like him, we can truly say that we are beginning to know him.* [Arthur R. Bassett, "He Has Been There Before Me", *Ensign*, July, 1975, 24]

To have eternal life, we must comprehend the Savior as He really is. To do this we must be like Him. If we are not like Him we cannot truly know Him. To the extent that we are not perfect as He is perfect, we do not know Him. "When he shall appear we shall be like him, for we shall see him as he is." [1 John 3:2; Moro. 7:49]

The promised gift of exaltation will probably not be lost because of a lack of knowledge or a testimony, but because of a failure to do God's will and become like He is. We will fail because we have not lived true to the knowledge we have. We may know the gospel is true and profess that eternal life is our goal, but fail because we lack the desire and the motivation to live as we know we should.

In human endeavors it is the will and desire to achieve that brings success rather than great ability. Untalented individuals, and even those with severe handicaps, can achieve success when highly motivated; while those with more ability fail because they lack motivation. This is even truer in spiritual endeavors. Once we bring to the Savior a burning desire to do His will, our spiritual powers are not limited by our natural abilities, but are multiplied through the grace of God. Our desire is the catalyst, and the power of God produces the "mighty change" in our lives.

> *Yea, come unto Christ, and be perfected in him, and deny yourselves of all ungodliness; and if ye shall deny yourselves of all ungodliness, and love God with all your might, mind and strength, then is his grace sufficient for you, that by his grace ye may be perfect in Christ; and if by the grace of God ye are perfect in Christ, ye can in nowise deny the power of God. [Moro. 10:32]*

The key to gain eternal life is to acquire that motivation which will insure that we will be totally obedient to the gospel plan. Is there something that will give us a consistent, all consuming desire to keep the commandments of God and do his will? Can it be discovered and acquired?

The work and glory of God is to bring to pass the immortality and eternal life of man. [Moses 1:39] The gospel plan was designed and adopted to accomplish these purposes. Heavenly Father and Jesus Christ have a great love for us. They have a great desire to help us obey the gospel and become like Them. However, the purposes of God for us cannot be accomplished without the exercise of our free agency in obedience to the gospel.

The great challenge our Heavenly Father, the Savior, and the prophets have had through all gospel dispensations is how, within the limits of our free agency, to secure obedience to God's commandments.

This is a common theme that runs through all of the scriptures and the exhortations of the living prophets. The gospel themes do not change from age to age—keep the commandments, live the gospel, do the will of God. The urging, the pleading, the exhorting to keep the commandments never cease. God is constantly striving to increase our desire to be obedient, and uses every means at his command.

> *How oft have I called upon you by the mouth of my servants, and by the ministering of angels, and by mine own voice, and by the voice of thunderings, and by the voice of lightnings, and by the voice of tempests, and by the voice of earthquakes, and great hailstorms, and by the voice of famines and pestilences of every kind, and by the great sound of a trump, and by the voice of judgment, and by the voice of mercy all the day long, and by the voice of glory and honor and the riches of eternal life, and would have saved you with an everlasting salvation, but ye would not! [D&C 43:25]*

The Savior understands that we are in different stages of spiritual responsiveness. Accordingly, He uses different kinds of motivation to help us, through the exercise of our free agency, to obey the commandments. Three kinds of gospel motivation are revealed in the scriptures—fear, duty and reward, and charity or the pure love of Christ. These three kinds of motivation, when used in the scriptures or by living prophets, may not be mutually exclusive. Elements of each may be found in any given exhortation by the prophets of God to obey the commandments.

These three types of gospel motivation can be considered as distinct levels of spiritual motivation, with fear being the lowest and charity the highest. These levels of gospel motivation can be differentiated on at least two bases: first, the motivational power, both as to intensity and duration; and second, the degree to which spiritual change is produced within an individual.

Fear has little consistent and lasting motivational strength, whereas charity has unlimited motivational power both as to intensity and duration. Obeying the gospel because of fear produces minimal spiritual change in an individual primarily because the motivation is external.

Obedience because of charity produces tremendous spiritual growth in one's character because the motivation is internalized. Obedience to gospel principles because of duty and reward has a motivational power and impact somewhere between that of fear and charity, but it alone cannot produce in a person those celestial personality traits necessary for exaltation. The fundamental importance of charity to the acquisition of eternal life is apparent when one understands and harmonizes the following scriptures:

> *And, if you keep my commandments and endure to the end you shall have eternal life, which gift is the greatest of all the gifts of God. [D&C 14:7]*

> *Wherefore, the wicked are rejected from the righteous, and also from that tree of life,*

whose fruit is most precious and most desirable above all other fruits; yea, and it is the greatest of all the gifts of God. [1 Nephi 15:36]

Yea, he saith: Come unto me and ye shall partake of the fruit of the tree of life; yea, ye shall eat and drink of the bread and the water of life freely. [Alma 5:34]

And it came to pass that I beheld that the rod of iron, which my father had seen, was the word of God, which led to the fountain of living waters, or to the tree of life; which waters are a representation of the love of God; and I also beheld that the tree of life was a representation of the love of God. [1 Nephi 11:25]

The gift of eternal life is the greatest of all the gifts of God, and also the fruit of the tree of life or the love of God or charity is the greatest of all the gifts of God. There is no contradiction between these scriptures. The key to a treasure is equal to the treasure itself. Charity, the pure love of Christ, is the key to eternal life and therefore the key and the ultimate treasure are both the greatest gifts of God.

The challenge we face is to move spiritually to the highest level of gospel motivation, to that of charity or the pure love of Christ—to move from obedience because of fear or because of duty and reward, to obedience and service because of charity. Many who would be called disciples of Christ can rightly say that they are not "hardhearted and stiff-necked" and have spiritually advanced from the motivational level of fear to that of duty and reward. But the real challenge is to move from that level of gospel motivation to that of charity or the pure love of Christ. Many who serve because of duty and reward have yet to feel the sweetness and power that comes from obedience and service because of charity. It is this level of gospel motivation which we should seek with all diligence. This motivation will sustain us and impel us to keep the commandments and do the will of God, for charity never faileth. Obedience and service because of the pure love of Christ will assuredly develop in our own being the Christ-like personality traits necessary for our exaltation.

CHAPTER FOUR

FEAR AS A GOSPEL MOTIVATING FORCE

Can fear of physical destruction in mortality or punishment after death motivate people to obey the commandments of God? Even so, we may question whether our Heavenly Father uses such fear motivation to get His children to be righteous and keep His commandments. Fear motivation means the threat of physical destruction or harm to person or property in this life or punishment after death. Book of Mormon scriptures illustrate the use of this type of motivation. Prophetic pronouncements of the physical destruction of the Nephites was a recurring theme.

> *And it came to pass that the prophets of the Lord did threaten the people of Nephi, according to the word of God, that if they did not keep the commandments, but should fall into transgression, they should be destroyed from off the face of the land. [Jarom 1:10]*

> *And the Lord God said unto me: They*

> *[Lamanites] shall be a scourge unto thy seed, to stir them up in remembrance of me; and inasmuch as they will not remember me, and hearken unto my words, they shall scourge them even unto destruction.* [2 Nephi 5:25]

The threat of physical destruction and eternal torment to motivate the Nephites to be obedient is bluntly expressed by Enos:

> *And there were exceedingly many prophets among us. And the people were a stiffnecked people, hard to understand. And there was nothing save it was exceeding harshness, preaching and prophesying of wars, and contentions, and destructions, and continually reminding them of death and the duration of eternity, and the judgments and the power of God, and all these things—stirring them up continually to keep them in the fear of the Lord. I say there was nothing short of these things, and exceeding great plainness of speech, would keep them from going down speedily to destruction. And after this manner do I write concerning them.* [Enos 1:22,23]

The use of fear as a motivational force is illustrated by the scriptural phrases of "endless torment" or "eternal damnation." The Book of Mormon prophets used the doctrine of "eternal punishment" to motivate the Nephites to obey the commandments of God.

> *And according to the power of justice,*

for justice cannot be denied, ye must go away into that lake of fire and brimstone, whose flames are unquenchable, and whose smoke ascendeth up forever and ever, which lake of fire and brimstone is endless torment. [Jacob 6:10]

And if they be evil they are consigned to an awful view of their own guilt and abominations, which doth cause them to shrink from the presence of the Lord into a state of misery and endless torment, from whence they can no more return; therefore they have drunk damnation to their own souls.

And their torment is as a lake of fire and brimstone, whose flames are unquenchable, and whose smoke ascendeth up forever and ever. Thus hath the Lord commanded me. Amen. [Mosiah 3:25,27]

Therefore, if that man repenteth not, and remaineth and dieth an enemy to God, the demands of divine justice do awaken his immortal soul to a lively sense of his own guilt, which doth cause him to shrink from the presence of the Lord, and doth fill his breast with guilt, and pain, and anguish, which is like an unquenchable fire, whose flame ascendeth up forever and ever.

And now I say unto you, that mercy hath no claim on that man; therefore his final doom is to endure a never-ending torment. [Mosiah 2:38,39]

The ordinary meaning of the phrases "eternal torment" or "eternal punishment" would be that such punishment endures forever, thereby having a strong motivational effect on the people to be obedient. The intended motivational impact of these phrases was explained to Joseph Smith as follows:

> *Nevertheless, it is not written that there shall be no end to this torment, but it is written endless torment.*
>
> *Again, it is written eternal damnation; wherefore it is more express than other scriptures,* ***that it might work upon the hearts of the children of men, altogether for my name's glory.***
>
> *Wherefore, I will explain unto you this mystery, for it is meet unto you to know even as mine apostles.*
>
> *I speak unto you that are chosen in this thing, even as one, that you may enter into my rest.*
>
> *For, behold, the mystery of godliness, how great is it! For, behold, I am endless, and the punishment which is given from my hand is endless punishment, for Endless is my name. Wherefore—*
>
> *Eternal punishment is God's punishment.*
>
> *Endless punishment is God's punish-*

ment. [D&C 19:6-12] [Emphasis added]

Those who will suffer eternal punishment or God's punishment are those who have not accepted Jesus Christ and repented of their sins. They will suffer for their individual sins even as Jesus Christ suffered.

> *For behold, I, God, have suffered these things for all, that they might not suffer if they would repent;*
>
> *But if they would not repent they must suffer even as I;*
>
> *Which suffering caused myself, even God, the greatest of all, to tremble because of pain, and to bleed at every pore, and to suffer both body and spirit—and would that I might not drink the bitter cup and shrink— [D&C 19:16-18]*

However, after they have paid the price of their sins, after justice has been satisfied, they will inherit a kingdom of glory, either the telestial or terrestrial glory depending on their individual merit.

The prophetic statements in the Book of Mormon that disobedience would result in the destruction of the Nephite civilization with death and eternal torment or punishment hereafter had no lasting motivational impact on the Nephites. In times of peace, security, and prosperity, the satisfaction of physical needs and desires were more real. The fear of destruction by the Lamanites or of some form of punishment after death seemed remote and irrelevant. The immediate satisfaction produced by material things and the pleasures of the flesh were more enticing.

The constant cyclical pattern among the Nephites of obedience, blessings and prosperity, followed by complacency, disobedience, and then wars or famine illustrate the fleeting nature of such motivation.

When the commandments of God are obeyed because of fear of physical destruction or eternal punishment, the focus of the individual is on one's self, his own comfort and happiness. There is little or no genuine concern for others. Obedience does not come from wanting to be obedient or helping others but derives from one's own physical or psychological comforts. Such obedience produces little, if any, personal spiritual growth. If motivation is external, righteous behavior falters and soon disappears when the outside stimulus or motivation is removed. Righteous behavior will not persist unless the very nature and character of a person is changed.

For some of God's children, those who as Enos described as "a stiffnecked people, hard to understand", obedience can begin through the motivation of fear of physical destruction or eternal punishment. Hopefully some individual spiritual growth can be started so that appeals to duty and charity will motivate greater obedience and bring greater and more lasting spiritual change.

CHAPTER FIVE

DUTY AND REWARD AS A GOSPEL MOTIVATING FORCE

The Savior frequently motivates us to be obedient by appeals to duty and promises of rewards or blessings. Duty and reward are reciprocal. We do our duty and receive the promised reward. We fail to do our duty and there is no promised blessing.

> *There is a law, irrevocably decreed in heaven before the foundation of this world, upon which all blessings are predicated—*
>
> *And when we obtain any blessing from God, it is by obedience to that law upon which it is predicated. [D&C 130:20-21]*
>
> *I, the Lord, am bound when ye do what I say; but when ye do not what I say, ye have no promise. [D&C 82:10]*

Appeals to do our duty and reiterations of the promised rewards are repeated throughout the scriptures and are a constant theme of the living prophets.

We are urged to do our duty both because we have promised to do so and because if we do, we will receive blessings in this life and in the life hereafter.

All men who know the commandments of God are under an obligation to obey. The Spirit of Christ is given to enable them to discern good from evil. [Moro. 7:16] However, the Savior knows that if individuals are placed under a specific covenant, promise, or duty to keep His commandments, His ability to motivate His children to be obedient will be greatly increased. Appeals to duty with the attendant promise of rewards or blessings are powerful motivating forces. The members of Christ's Church in all dispensations have been a covenant people. Baptism, ordination to the priesthood, the temple endowment and celestial marriage are sacred covenants, voluntarily assumed obligations to obey the celestial laws of obedience, sacrifice and consecration, with the promised blessing of eternal life. [Bruce R. McConkie, "Obedience, Consecration and Sacrifice", *Ensign*, May 1975, 50]

Gospel covenants and ordinances help motivate us to obey the commandments. The sacred and symbolic nature of the ordinances impress upon our minds the seriousness of the obligations which we have taken upon us.

Through the ordinances we take upon ourselves the name of Christ, the Son of God. We become sons and daughters of God; we receive the promise that as we move from grace to grace we can, as did the Savior, receive of the fulness of the Father's glory. [D&C 93:14-20]

By partaking of the sacrament, members of the Church renew their baptismal covenant to keep the commandments with the promise that obedience brings the blessing of the constant companionship of the Holy Ghost. The scriptures are replete with reminders of our duty to obey the commandments as we have promised and the rewards which obedience will bring:

> *Wherefore, now let every man learn his duty, and to act in the office in which he is appointed, in all diligence. He that is slothful shall not be counted worthy to stand, and he that learns not his duty and shows himself not approved shall not be counted worthy to stand. Even so. Amen. [D&C 107:99-100]*
>
> *For verily I say unto you, blessed is he that keepeth my commandments, whether in life or in death; and he that is faithful in tribulation, the reward of the same is greater in the kingdom of heaven.* [D&C 58:2]
>
> *But learn that he who doeth the works of righteousness shall receive his reward, even peace in this world, and eternal life in the world to come. [D&C 59:23]*
>
> *And thus, if ye are faithful ye shall be laden with many sheaves, and crowned with honor, and glory, and immortality, and eternal life. [D&C 75:5]*

Obeying the commandments of God because of duty or a sense of obligation or a desire to gain a reward in this life or hereafter has limitations, both as to moral quality, motivational force, and the spiritual growth received. When we keep the commandments or serve others only out of a sense of duty or desire for reward, the focus of our obedience may be upon ourselves and not because of a genuine concern or love for others. One can serve out of a sense of duty and have little or no real concern for others. The service can be mechanical, impersonal—the accomplishment of a task merely so that we can report that it has been accomplished. We serve because we have promised to do so; it is our responsibility. We must be true to ourselves. To do less than our duty would be to lower ourselves in our own eyes or in the eyes of our peers. We do not want to appear to be less than we have promised outwardly. We view ourselves as righteous and obedient; to retain our own self-image, we obey the commandments.

When we serve only because of duty, our attitude toward those we serve is often not right. We may have negative, unkind, or self-righteous feelings toward those we serve or sometimes an attitude of superiority that the objects of our service are not really appreciative or worthy of our efforts. Such service rarely blesses the lives of others.

Also, service because of duty alone usually places outer limits or boundaries on our service. We are willing to go so far or do so much, but no more. Because the scope of the performance of our duty is limited, so also will be the promised blessing. Our service is "first mile" service, not "second or third mile service."

Keeping the commandments only because of duty or for the promised reward lacks high moral quality and many times does not bring the anticipated spiritual blessings. It has a limited effect in developing Christ-like virtues in one's character. The great paradox of the gospel is that if we keep the commandments only for the promised blessings and rewards, we do not receive them; if we keep the commandments because of the love of others and to bless their lives, the promised blessings come.

> *Then said Jesus unto his disciples, If any man will come after me, let him deny himself, and take up his cross, and follow me.*
>
> *For whosoever will save his life shall lose it: and whosoever will lose his life for my sake shall find it. [Matt. 16:24-25]*

Obedience to God's commandments and service which does not produce in us Christ-like qualities will not result in our obtaining eternal life. The following scripture reminds us of this important concept:

> *Verily I say unto you, it is not everyone that saith unto me, Lord, Lord, that shall enter into the kingdom of heaven; but he that doeth the will of my Father who is in heaven.*
>
> *For the day soon cometh, that men shall come before me to judgment, to be judged according to their works.*
>
> *And many will say unto me in that day, Lord, Lord, have we not prophesied in thy name; and in thy name cast out devils, and in thy name done many wonderful works?*
>
> *And then will I say, ye never knew me: depart from me ye that work iniquity.* [Matt. 7:30-33, Inspired Version]

This scripture can best be understood if we

comprehend the nature of the reward of eternal life. President Lorenzo Snow said: "Godliness cannot be conferred but must be acquired." [Eliza R. Snow, *Biography and Family Record of Lorenzo Snow* (Salt Lake City: Deseret News Co., 1884), 193] Good deeds, good acts, the keeping of the commandments in and of themselves do not bring forth the promised blessing, namely the acquisition of godliness. God cannot confer this upon anyone as a reward for good acts or deeds. We do not "earn" the right to become as God.

Godliness is developed from within. As we acquire the Savior's qualities and attributes, we become as He is. A lifetime of sacrament meeting attendance, the payment of tithes and offerings, service as a Relief Society president, or quorum or stake president, or ordinance work for our ancestors may not produce in us the Christ-like qualities necessary for celestial glory. The blessing of eternal life may elude us if we only serve because of duty or reward. Our service will not have produced in us a celestial personality. One is reminded of the following scripture:

> *For notwithstanding they die, they also shall rise again, a spiritual body.*
>
> ***They who are of a celestial spirit shall receive the same body which was a natural body;*** *even ye shall receive your bodies, and your glory shall be that glory by which your bodies are quickened.*
>
> *Ye who are quickened by a portion of the celestial glory shall then receive of the same, even a fulness.* [D&C 88:27-29](Emphasis added)

The motivation to be obedient because of duty and reward will not and cannot sustain us. It lacks the constant and powerful force necessary to motivate us to do and to endure those things which will be required of us in our quest for exaltation. We need a stronger gospel motivational force than duty and reward to overcome the trials, afflictions, challenges and materialistic enticements of this life. To truly serve and bless the lives of the unlovable, the rebellious, those who intentionally hurt and speak evil of us, the unappreciative, the proud, and those with whom we would rather not associate, will take something more powerful. Charity, the pure love of Christ will be required.

However, notwithstanding what has been said, we should not despair; obedience because of duty and reward will lead us along the gospel path of true spiritual growth and perfection. Hopefully, as we struggle and strive to do our duty, gradually our desires will change. The desires of the natural man will be replaced with divine desires; we will become like Jesus Christ with His attributes and feelings. The motivational force of duty and reward will lead us to acquire the greatest motivational force of all—that of charity, the pure love of Christ.

CHAPTER SIX

CHARITY, THE PURE LOVE OF CHRIST, AS A GOSPEL MOTIVATING FORCE

The most powerful motivating force to do good and to keep the commandments of God is charity, the pure love of Christ. It is more powerful, more intense, more constant and enduring than the motivational forces of fear of punishment, or promises of rewards, or appeals to duty.

When the Savior began his mortal ministry, he spoke of the two great commandments:

> *Thou shalt love the Lord thy God with all thy heart, and with all thy soul, and with all thy mind.*
>
> *This is the first and great commandment.*
>
> *And the second is like unto it. Thou shalt love thy neighbor as thyself. [Matt. 22:37-39]*

The standard, or quality of love for others was to love them as you love yourself. However, at the Feast of the Passover when the Savior introduced the sacrament to His disciples just prior to His suffering in the Garden of Gethsemane, He gave his disciples a new commandment and a higher standard of how they should love one another.

> *A new commandment I give unto you, That ye love one another; as I have loved you, that ye also love one another.*
>
> *By this shall all men know that ye are my disciples, if ye have love one to another. [John 13:34-35]*

Charity is a divine gift. We do not possess it in our own human nature. We may love our spouse, our children or a dear and close friend with feelings of deep and intense love. However, these feelings of love are but shadows when compared with charity, the pure love of Christ. Mortals cannot develop this divine love without an endowment of power from God.

Charity is that quality of love that motivated God, our Eternal Father, and His Son Jesus Christ in proposing and executing the great plan of eternal salvation. As Elder Neal A. Maxwell has said: "Indeed, while God's great plan of redemption was made feasible by His omniscience and His omnipotence, it was made inevitable because of His perfect love for us!" [Neal A. Maxwell, *All These Things Shall Give Thee Experience,* (Salt Lake City: Deseret Book Co., 1979), 128]

Jesus Christ "so loved the world that he gave his own life, that as many as would believe might become the sons of God." [D&C 34:3)]

> *And again, I remember that thou hast said that thou hast loved the world, even unto the laying down of thy life for the world, that thou mightest take it again to prepare a place for the children of men.*
>
> *And now I know that this love which thou has had for the children of men is charity; wherefore, except men shall have charity they cannot inherit that place which thou hast prepared in the mansions of thy Father.* [Ether 12:33,34]

Christ's pure love for each of us motivated Him to suffer the incomprehensible agony of the atonement when He sweat blood from every pore of His body. Because of this love, the Savior, as He hung on the cross at Calvary, was able to say: "Father forgive them; for they know not what they do." [Luke 23:34]

The scriptures have always emphasized the singular importance of charity. Paul and Moroni declared that without charity we are nothing, without charity our good acts do not profit us. And of faith, hope and charity, charity is the greatest of all. [1 Cor. 13; Moro. 7:46]

The interpretation given to Nephi of Lehi's vision of the tree of life helps us to understand the importance of charity.

> *And the angel said unto me: Behold the Lamb of God, yea, even the Son of the Eternal Father! Knowest thou the meaning of the tree which thy father saw?*

> *And I answered him, saying: Yea, it is the love of God, which sheddeth itself abroad in the hearts of the children of men; wherefore, it is the most desirable above all things.*
>
> *And he spake unto me, saying: Yea, and the most joyous to the soul.*
>
> *And after he had said these words, he said unto me: Look! And I looked, and I beheld the Son of God going forth among the children of men; and I saw many fall down at his feet and worship him.*
>
> *And it came to pass that I beheld that the rod of iron, which my father had seen, was the word of God, which led to the fountain of living waters, or to the tree of life; which waters are a representation of the love of God; and I also beheld that the tree of life was a representation of the love of God. [1 Nephi 11:21-25]*
>
> *Wherefore, the wicked are rejected from the righteous, and also from that tree of life, whose fruit is most precious and most desirable above all other fruits; yea, and it is the greatest of all the gifts of God. And thus I spake unto my brethren. Amen. [1 Nephi 15:36]*

Charity is Christ's pure love for us. It is the quality of love which we should have for the Savior and for every other person, and which we must have if we would gain eternal life. We should be both a recipient and a giver of the pure love of Christ. Nephi declared that the love of God or charity is "the most joyous to the soul" and "the most desirable above all things" and "the greatest of all the gifts of God."

The pure love of Christ encompasses ultimate joy or happiness. Joy or happiness is the end of our existence, "for men are that they might have joy." [2 Nephi 2:25] As we receive the pure love of Christ and give to it to others, we experience great joy.

> *As the Father hath loved me, so have I loved you: continue ye in my love.*
>
> *If ye keep my commandments, ye shall abide in my love; even as I have kept my Father's commandments, and abide in his love.*
>
> *These things have I spoken unto you, that my joy might remain in you, and that your joy might be full.*
>
> *This is my commandment, That ye love one another, as I have loved you. [John 15:9-12]*

The relationship between charity and joy is illustrated in the account of Christ's visit to the Nephites after his resurrection.

Jesus had borne His testimony to the Nephites that He was the Son of God. He had taught them the necessity of baptism, the truths of the Sermon on the Mount and that the law of Moses was fulfilled in Him. He told the people that they should ponder and pray about the things which He had taught them and that He would visit them the following day.

And it came to pass that when Jesus had thus spoken, he cast his eyes round about again on the multitude, and beheld that they were in tears, and did look steadfastly upon him as if they would ask him to tarry a little longer with them.

And he said unto them: Behold, my bowels are filled with compassion [love] towards you. [3 Nephi 17:5,6]

Jesus then asked the Nephites to bring all of their sick, lame, blind, and dumb and "he did heal them everyone as they were brought forth unto him." [3 Nephi 17:9]

And no tongue can speak, neither can there be written by any man, neither can the hearts of men conceive so great and marvelous things as we both saw and heard Jesus speak; and no one can conceive of the joy which filled our souls at the time we heard him pray for us unto the Father.

And it came to pass that when Jesus had made an end of praying unto the Father, he arose; but so great was the joy of the multitude that they were overcome.

And it came to pass that Jesus spake unto them, and bade them arise.

And they arose from the earth, and he said unto them: Blessed are ye because of your faith. And now behold, my joy is full.

> *And when he had said these words, he wept, and the multitude bare record of it, and he took their little children, one by one, and blessed them, and prayed unto the Father for them.*
>
> *And when he had done this he wept again. [3 Nephi 17:17-22]*

In the foregoing account, Christ exhibited His pure love for the people, who as recipients, felt His great love. As Christ experienced this pure love for the people, He declared: "Behold, my joy is full." The joy of the multitude was so great that they were overcome, that "no one can conceive of the joy which filled their souls". [3 Nephi 17:17,20]

Associated with the incomprehensible joy is an all consuming desire to seek and retain it through righteous living and service to others. The feelings associated with charity are two-fold: first, an overwhelming feeling of great joy and elation, and second, an all consuming desire to serve and bless the lives of others. As Nephi expressed: "He hath filled me with his love, even unto the consuming of my flesh", [2 Nephi 4:21] and "for I am filled with the power of God, even unto the consuming of my flesh." [1 Nephi 17:48] Nephi describes both the love of God and the power of God with the identical words.

The pure love of Christ is the greatest motivating force in our lives for righteous living and service to others. It is "the most joyous to the soul" and "the most desirable above all things," not only because of the joy which one feels, but because of the great desire and power it instills in one to serve and bless the lives of others.

The motivational power of the love of God is illustrated by Lehi's account of his vision of the tree of life.

> *And as I partook of the fruit thereof it filled my soul with exceeding great joy; wherefore, I began to be desirous that my family should partake of it also; for I knew that it was desirable above all other fruit. [1 Nephi 8:12]*

As Lehi partook of the fruit of the tree of life (the love of God) he experienced a great joy and also a desire to bless the lives of his family. Enos had a similar desire to bless the lives of others after having felt the love of God in answer to his earnest prayer. [Enos 1:9)]

The love of God in Lehi's vision was represented or symbolized by the "tree of life" and the "fountain of living waters." These are suggestive of a never ending source of power, strength, vitality and action—in other words, a divine motivational force. Charity will overcome all trials, afflictions and tribulations, all obstacles. Charity will endure and continue to motivate us to do the will of God. When other things fail, charity will not. It will continue to impel us toward celestial perfection.

Apostle Melvin J. Ballard's account of a dream in which he saw the Savior also illustrates the tremendous motivational force that comes from experiencing the pure love of Christ:

> *After a season of prayer and rejoicing I was informed that I should have the privilege*

> *of entering into one of those rooms, to meet a glorious Personage, and as I entered the door, I saw, seated on a raised platform, the most glorious Being my eyes have ever beheld or that I ever conceived existed in all the eternal worlds. As I approached to be introduced, he arose and stepped towards me with extended arms, and he smiled as he softly spoke my name. If I shall live to be a million years old, I shall never forget that smile. He took me into his arms and kissed me, pressed me to his bosom, and blessed me, until the marrow of my bones seemed to melt! When he had finished, I knelt at his feet, and, as I bathed them with my tears and kisses, I saw the prints of the nails in the feet of the Redeemer of the world. The feeling that I had in the presence of him who hath all things in his hands, to have his love, his affection, and his blessing was such that if I ever can receive that of which I had but a foretaste, I would give all that I am, all that I ever hope to be, to feel what I then felt.* [Bryant S. Hinckley, *Sermons and Missionary Service of Melvin J. Ballard*, (Salt Lake City: Deseret Book Co., 1949), 155-56]

Elder George F. Richards, when President of the Quorum of the Twelve, recounted a somewhat similar dream:

> *In this dream I was in the presence of my Savior as he stood mid-air. He spoke no word to me, but my love for him was such that I have not words to explain. I know that no*

> *mortal man can love the Lord as I experienced that love for the Savior unless God reveals it to him. I would have remained in his presence, but there was a power drawing me away from him. As a result of that dream, I had this feeling that no matter what might be required of my hands, what the gospel might entail unto me, I would do what I should be asked to do even to the laying down of my life. If only I can be with my Savior and have that same sense of love that I had in that dream, it will be the goal of my existence, the desire of my life.* [General Conference, October 1896, *The Deseret Weekly,* October 31, 1896, vol. 53, 610]

What great power comes from experiencing the pure love of Christ in our lives! We in turn have a pure love for the Savior and for all of our Heavenly Father's children. Our confidence waxes strong in the presence of God as we feel His love. We have the ability that comes from the exercise of great faith to pull down the powers of heaven as we minister to those over whom we have been given responsibility. We comprehend the grand design which God has for us. We truly see our own potential as sons and daughters of God and the potential of all those about us. No longer are we limited in our Church service by thoughts and concerns of reward or blessings, or the performance of our duty. These are all swept away, subsumed in an all consuming joy and desire to lift, serve and bless all those around us, irrespective of position, degree of righteousness, desirability, or attractiveness. We truly become Christ-like because we are now serving as He served. We are now capable of blessing the lives of others as He did. As we continue, eventually we will become as He is, and we shall see or "know" the Savior as He truly is, for we shall be like Him. [1 John 3:2)] The gift of eternal life may then be ours because we have come to really know the Savior.

CHAPTER SEVEN

OBTAINING CHARITY

The pure love of Christ is a gift from God and as all heavenly gifts, it is only dispensed in accordance with certain divine conditions and principles. As Moroni declared:

> *Wherefore, my beloved brethren, if ye have not charity, ye are nothing, for charity never faileth. Wherefore, cleave unto charity, which is the greatest of all, for all things must fail—*
>
> *But charity is the pure love of Christ, and it endureth forever; and whoso is found possessed of it at the last day, it shall be well with him.*
>
> *Wherefore, my beloved brethren, pray unto the Father with all the energy of heart, that ye may be filled with this love, which he hath bestowed upon all who are true followers of his Son, Jesus Christ; that ye may become the sons of God; that when he shall appear we*

> *shall be like him, for we shall see him as he is; that we may have this hope; that we may be purified even as he is pure. Amen.* [Moro. 7:46-48]

Charity is a gift of God, but it is only given to those who have prepared themselves to receive it. In this regard, it is like the gift of the Holy Ghost or the gift of eternal life. The gifts of God are only given to those who satisfy the eternal conditions which govern their bestowal.

What are the conditions suggested by the scriptures which must be met to obtain the gift of charity? What must I do to receive this most precious gift?

A. DESIRE CHARITY

The first step to receiving the gift of charity is to have a determined desire to obtain it. We must make a conscious decision to acquire this gift. Perhaps at first it is no more than a desire to have a desire. After the affirmative decision to acquire charity is made, we must do all we can to strengthen this desire until it is an all consuming desire, until we "hunger and thirst" after charity. Then God will fill us with His love because it is an eternal gospel principle that God grants us the righteous desires of our hearts.

> *And it came to pass that after [Enos] had prayed and labored with all diligence, the Lord said unto me: I will grant unto thee according to thy desires, because of thy faith. [Enos 1:12]*

The Savior said "even as you desire of me so it shall be done unto you" and "all things whatsoever you desire of me, which are pertaining unto things of righteousness, in faith believing in me that you shall receive." [D&C 11:8,14] This gospel principle is illustrated by the desires of Peter and John the Beloved expressed to the Savior just prior to His ascension unto heaven. Peter desired that he might speedily go to the Savior in His kingdom, but John desired to tarry in mortality until the Savior's second coming in order to bring souls to salvation. Both desires were righteous and were granted by the Savior.

> *Verily I say unto you, ye shall both have according to your desires, for ye both joy in that which ye have desired. [D&C 7:8]*

If you would receive the gift of charity, you must then first desire it with all your heart.

B. CONSISTENT MIGHTY PRAYER

As Moroni has counseled, we must "pray unto the Father with all energy of heart, that [we] may be filled with this [charity]." [Moro. 7:48] Through prayer, our desire for the gift of charity is manifest. The depth and intensity of our prayers is an accurate measure of our desire. A few quick moments in prayer each day will not effect the necessary change in our lives and belies any earnest desire.

As Enos, we must go to the Lord in "mighty prayer and supplication." We struggle with the Lord to grant us the righteous desires of our heart. As we wrestle with the Lord in mighty prayer, we offer our sacrifice of a broken heart and a contrite spirit. We bare our souls and acknowledge our total dependence on the Savior. We plead for mercy and forgiveness. Our spirits are cleansed and purified, and finally our spirits fill and enlarge as we feel in some measure the pure love of Christ descend upon us. We come to know that our sins are forgiven through the great love of the Savior in suffering for our own personal sins. As we feel His love for us, our hearts swell and expand with this same love for others.

Mighty prayer must be a consistent part of our daily life, for Moroni counseled that the perfect love of God "endureth by diligence unto prayer." [Moro. 8:26] Through mighty prayer we gain the power to change our very nature, to have the image of Christ engraven upon our countenance. We can become good by ourselves, but to become Christ-like, to have the pure love of Christ, we need the power of Christ. This power is gained through mighty prayer. Not only should we have consistent daily prayer, but there should be special times of fasting, meditation and extended prayer; times when the spirit bears witness of the reality of our divine destiny, and times when our only purpose is to gain a closer feeling of love and kinship to our Heavenly Father and Jesus Christ. Through mighty prayer we can be blessed with the gift of charity.

C. SURRENDER YOUR AGENCY TO GOD

If we would have the pure love of Christ, we must follow completely the example of the Savior in doing the will of His Father. The Savior said: "I am Jesus

Christ; I came by the will of the Father, and I do his will." [D&C 19:24] We must do the will of the Father in all things. His desires for us are perfect, our desires are imperfect. He knows what course of action will perfect, sanctify and celestialize our lives. We know what we want, but our Heavenly Father, from an eternal perspective, knows what we need.

We must take our free agency, that which is coeternal with God, the only thing which is truly our own and which is the essence of our life and existence and give it absolutely to God. We give Him the one gift that He would never take from us. [Boyd K. Packer, "Obedience", *B.Y.U. Speeches of the Year*, December 7, 1971, 3,4] We hold back nothing. We reserve no small domain in which our will is supreme. We eliminate from our spirit every remaining vestige of willful disobedience or rebellion. This must be done not grudgingly but in a spirit of gratitude and complete trust. Having completely surrendered our will to our Heavenly Father, we follow the perfect example of the Savior. We are then prepared to receive and give the pure love of Christ.

D. FEAST UPON THE WORDS OF CHRIST

To determine God's will for us in our individual lives, we must continually feast upon the words of Christ:

> *Wherefore, I said unto you, feast upon the words of Christ; for behold, the words of Christ will tell you all things what ye should do. [2 Nephi 32:3]*

We must study and ponder the scriptures and their meaning in our individual lives. We must gain a love for the scriptures as did Nephi: "For my soul delighteth in the scriptures, and my heart pondereth them." [2 Nephi 4:15] If we would become like God and have the pure love of Christ, we must have God-like thoughts. For as a man thinketh in his heart, so is he.

> *A noble and Godlike character is not a thing of favor or chance, but is the natural result of continued effort in right thinking, the effect of long-cherished association with Godlike thoughts.* [James Allen, *As a Man Thinketh* (Salt Lake City: Bookcraft), 8]

We cannot know Jesus Christ, we cannot know of His pure love unless our thoughts are focused on Him and His life.

> *For how knoweth a man the master whom he has not served, and who is a stranger unto him, and is far from the thoughts and intents of his heart? [Mosiah 5:13]*

The scriptures bring the focus of our thoughts back to the Savior, back to spiritual values. The Holy Ghost again bears witness to our spirit of eternal truths. We are recommitted to obey the commandments.

In today's world we are bombarded incessantly

with stimulating appeals for the gratification of our own physical and materialistic desires. The ideals of the world: money, sex, power, and physical pleasure are continually before us with ever increasing intensity. These worldly appeals overwhelm and soon crowd out the sweetness and gentleness of spiritual things and feelings of concern, compassion and tenderness for others.

We deceive ourselves if we think we can remain immune from the desires and attitudes of the world without the continuous fortification of the scriptures. The selfish, ego-centered, pleasure-seeking, and materialistic ideals of the world soon taint and discolor our souls unless we constantly immerse ourselves in the cleansing and living water of the scriptures.

If we would have the pure love of Christ, we must constantly study and ponder about it and the spiritual values related to it. The scriptures are the vehicle which the Lord has provided to so focus our thoughts. The word of God is the "rod of iron" which will lead us through the evil "mist of darkness" of the world to the tree of life, which is the love of God.

> *And it came to pass that I beheld that the rod of iron, which my father had seen, was the word of God, which led to the fountain of living waters, or to the tree of life; which waters are a representation of the love of God; and I also beheld that the tree of life was a representation of the love of God. [1 Nephi 11:25]*

E. APPLY THE "AS IF" PRINCIPLE

Some people are lovable; others are not. The

challenge is to love the unlovable, the unpleasant, the unattractive, the repulsive and, indeed, our enemies.

C.S. Lewis counseled us to apply the "as if" principle:

> *The rule for all of us is perfectly simple. Do not waste time bothering whether you 'love' your neighbour; act as if you did. As soon as we do this we find one of the great secrets. When you are behaving as if you loved someone, you will presently come to love him. If you injure someone you dislike, you will find yourself disliking him more. If you do him a good turn, you will find yourself disliking him less.... The difference between a Christian and a worldly man is not that the worldly man has only affections or 'likings' and the Christian has only 'charity.' The worldly man treats certain people kindly because he 'likes' them: the Christian, trying to treat every one kindly, finds himself liking more and more people as he goes on–including people he could not even have imagined himself liking at the beginning.* [C.S. Lewis, *Mere Christianity* (New York: Macmillan Publishing Co.) 116-17]

F. SEEK TO BLESS THE LIVES OF INDIVIDUALS

Snoopy, in the comic strip, "Peanuts" made the telling admission: "I love mankind; it's the people I can't stand." Charity is not an abstract love for mankind in general, but a compelling desire to lift and bless individual lives. The children of God are not saved in "bunches", but are saved one by one. This truth was taught by the Savior in the parable of the lost sheep. The true shepherd must leave the ninety and nine and go out into the wilderness and find the one lost sheep. By this, his true love is manifest to and understood by the one. The ninety-nine also understand more deeply the shepherd's love for them as they observe his love for the one lost sheep.

Charity demands care and concern for the spiritual needs of individuals. No better illustration of this quality of charity is found in the scriptures than Christ's ministration to the Nephites as "he took their little children, one by one, and blessed them." [3 Nephi 17:21)] It would have been easier, less time consuming, less bothersome for the Savior to have blessed the children as a group, but the pure love of Christ compelled the giving of individual blessings fashioned for individual needs. A person endowed with the pure love of Christ understands that individuals must first be perfected before families or groups can be prepared for celestial glory. The following experience of Elder Burke Peterson illustrates this principle:

> *Two weeks ago President Kimball passed me as we were rushing to a meeting. He stopped, took my hand, looked me in the eye, put away all of his other cares, and said simply, 'I'm sorry we're sometimes so busy. I guess I haven't told you lately how much I love you and appreciate you.' I felt his spirit; I believed him; my spirit soared to a new height.* [H. Burke Peterson, "The Daily Portion of Love", *Ensign*, May 1977, 68]

Charity requires our spiritual and emotional involvement with real people with real problems. Such personal involvement is emotionally, spiritually and physically draining. It requires time, patience, long suffering, a forgiving spirit, and an empathetic attitude free from judging or criticizing. It requires a special spiritual strength so as not to become people weary.

Charity also involves emotional risks: the risk of not being understood, or appreciated, or listened to, or having your heart broken as those you love turn away into paths of sin and sorrow.

> *There is no safe investment. To love at all is to be vulnerable. Love anything and your heart will certainly be wrung and possibly be broken. If you want to make sure of keeping it intact, you must give your heart to no one. Wrap it carefully round with hobbies and little luxuries; avoid all entanglements; lock it up safe in the casket or coffin of your selfishness.* [C.S. Lewis, *The Four Loves* (Glasgow, England: William Collins Son & Co., Ltd., 1960), 111]

The account of the sorrow of God as He viewed the wickedness of His children helps us appreciate the emotional risks in having charity for others. Enoch expressed wonderment as he saw the Lord weep for His children. The Lord explained:

> *Satan shall be their father, and misery shall be their doom; and the whole heavens shall weep over them, even all the workmanship of mine hands; wherefore should not the heavens weep, seeing these shall suffer?*

> *Wherefore, for this shall the heavens weep, yea, and all the workmanship of my hands...*
>
> *Wherefore Enoch knew, and looked upon their wickedness, and their misery, and wept and stretched forth his arms and his heart swelled wide as eternity; and his bowels yearned; and all eternity shook. [Moses 7:37,40,41]*

Charity, the pure love of Christ, is willing to suffer all things in order to bring one individual, precious, eternal soul back to the presence of God. Charity comprehends the individual worth of one child of God and is willing to pay the high price oft times required to bring that one child back to God.

G. COMPARE YOUR THOUGHTS AND FEELINGS WITH THOSE WHO HAVE CHARITY

There are many examples in the scriptures with which we can compare our own feelings and attitudes in order to measure our spiritual progress. The ultimate example, of course, is the Savior. The account of the Savior's ministry among the Nephites after His resurrection vividly illustrates Christ's pure love and can be used by us to determine in what measure we also have this love in our service to others. In this regard, chapter seventeen of Third Nephi should be read and studied often.

The Savior had ministered to those assembled and had instructed them to:

> *Ponder upon the things which I have said, and ask of the Father, in my name, that ye may understand, and prepare your minds for the morrow, and I come unto you again. [3 Nephi 17:3]*

The Savior told the multitude He must go to the lost tribes of Israel:

> *And it came to pass that when Jesus had thus spoken, he cast his eyes round about again on the multitude, and beheld they were in tears, and did look steadfastly upon him as if they would ask him to tarry a little longer with them.*
>
> *And he said unto them: Behold, my bowels are filled with compassion towards you. [3 Nephi 17:5,6]*

They brought forth all of their sick, lame, blind, and dumb and "he did heal them everyone as they were brought forth unto him." [3 Nephi 17:9] The Savior then knelt in prayer with the multitude:

> *And no tongue can speak, neither can there be written by any man, neither can the hearts of men conceive so great and marvelous things as we both saw and heard Jesus speak; and no one can conceive of the joy which filled our souls at the time we heard him pray for us unto the Father.*

> *And it came to pass that when Jesus had made an end of praying unto the Father, he arose; but so great was the joy of the multitude that they were overcome.*
>
> *And it came to pass that Jesus spake unto them, and bade them arise.*
>
> *And they arose from the earth, and he said unto them: Blessed are ye because of your faith. And now behold my joy is full.*
>
> *And when he had said these words, he wept, and the multitude bear record of it, and he took their little children, one by one, and blessed them, and prayed unto the Father for them.*
>
> *And when he had done this he wept again. [3 Nephi 17:17-22]*

One cannot read, study and ponder the foregoing scriptures without coming to a greater understanding of the pure love of Christ. The Holy Ghost can enlighten the mind and the heart to truly comprehend the depth and the breadth of the feelings of compassion and concern for others that is encompassed by the pure love of Christ. Our true feelings towards others can be compared with those of the Savior. Although such a comparison may be devastating, it is necessary. Before one can reach a destination, he must know what the destination is, what road he must travel, and where along the road he is.

The prophet Nephi had the gift of charity. In his final remarks, Nephi laments the unbelief, wickedness, ignorance, and stiffneckedness of men in refusing to accept a knowledge of God. He expresses charity for his people, the Jews, and the Gentiles:

> *For I pray continually for them by day, and mine eyes water my pillow by night, because of them; and I cry unto my God in faith, and I know that he will hear my cry. [2 Nephi 33:3]*

Nephi felt the love of God "unto the consuming of his flesh." [2 Nephi 4:21]

Alma expressed his love and concern for his brethren as follows:

> *And now, my brethren, I wish from the inmost part of my heart, yea, with great anxiety even unto pain, that ye would hearken unto my words ...[Alma 13:27]*

Moroni also experienced charity:

> *Behold, I speak with boldness, having authority from God; and I fear not what man can do; for perfect love casteth out all fear.*
>
> *And I am filled with charity, which is everlasting love; wherefore, all children are alike unto me; wherefore, I love little children with a perfect love; and they are all alike and partakers of salvation. [Moro. 8:16-17]*

Enoch had charity and when he saw the wickedness and misery of the children of God, he "wept and stretched forth his arms, and his bowels yearned; and all eternity shook." [Moses 7:41]

Comparing our own thoughts and feelings for others with those of the Savior and the great men of God both past and present will show us where we are and where we must travel to secure for ourselves the gift of charity.

H. STRIVE FOR PERFECTION IN THIS LIFE

"Be ye therefore perfect, even as your Father which is in heaven is perfect." [Matt. 5:48] Those who inherit the celestial kingdom "are they who are just men made perfect through Jesus the mediator of the new covenant." [D&C 76:69] President Spencer W. Kimball in commenting on the Savior's command to be perfect has said:

> *I would emphasize that the teachings of Christ that we should become perfect were not mere rhetoric. He meant literally that it is the right of mankind to become like the Father and like the Son having overcome human weaknesses and developed attributes of divinity. Because many individuals do not fully use the capacity that is theirs does nothing to negate the truth that they have the power to become Christlike.* [Spencer W. Kimball, "Hold Fast to the Iron Rod", *Ensign*, Nov. 1978, 6]

Each person could well ask himself the question,

"Am I seriously striving for perfection?" Or is it an ethereal concept that lacks any sense of reality in my personal life? Do we believe it is possible to approach perfection now, or is it merely an idealistic statement of a condition which may occur in the dim, eternal future?

To excel in any endeavor, or to become a champion, one must first convince himself that it is possible; that with enough desire, effort, struggle, and pain, the goal can be achieved. We have God's promise that we may become spiritually perfect. Christ will make spiritual champions of every person if that person will allow Him to do so, and unlike champion athletes, no inherent or natural talent is a prerequisite. Someone has expressed the thought that "no one is so low or deficient in spirituality that the gospel of Jesus Christ can not lift him to celestial glory." This is the genius of the atonement and grace of Jesus Christ. He is the great spiritual equalizer. He only requires our desire, our will, our obedience, and our work. A missionary once expressed it as follows: "With the help of Jesus Christ I can accomplish anything; I can become what I want to; I can become perfect."

The degree of perfection which we achieve in this life will certainly never be greater than our belief of what is possible. Perhaps many have never thought of trying to achieve perfection, or are content to be no better or worse than their friends or neighbors. We sometimes justify our action by the attitude, "Well, nobody is perfect." But our standard should be Jesus Christ, not the person next door. We should strive to bring our actions up to that standard, not find a standard that matches our action.

We cannot become totally perfect during mortality; however, no one compels us to sin. Our transgressions are a result of our own free will. Elder Boyd K. Packer, in addressing a group of mission presidents and their wives, stated: "I don't think any one of you is perfect. I don't know anyone who is. I know some few who are that close." [Boyd K. Packer, Seminar for New Mission Presidents, June 22, 1978]

We, too, can get that close to perfection.

The Prophet Joseph Smith taught the singular importance of the love of God:

> *Love is one of the chief characteristics of Deity, and ought to be manifested by those who aspire to be the sons of God. A man filled with the love of God is not content with blessing his family alone, but ranges through the whole world, anxious to bless the whole human race.* [Joseph Fielding Smith, *Teachings of the Prophet Joseph Smith*, (Salt Lake City: Deseret News Press, 3rd ed. 1942), 174]

Charity encompasses all other virtues: humility, patience, long suffering, kindness, mercy, forgiveness, gratitude and reverence. [1 Cor. 13:4-7] To the extent that we do not possess these other virtues, we are deficient in charity.

The opposite of charity is selfishness. All sin is but a manifestation of our selfishness. Dishonesty, lying, pride, slothfulness, immorality, ingratitude, anger, irreverence, love of money and power, are all evidence of our selfishness or lack of charity.

As we achieve perfection in one virtue, we move closer to the ideal of charity. Perfection in one area strengthens our resolve and increases our capacity to achieve perfection in another. This striving for perfection is illustrated by the feelings expressed by Nephi in 2 Nephi 4, the Psalm of Nephi:

> *Yea, my heart sorroweth because of my flesh; my soul grieveth because of mine iniquities.*
>
> *I am encompassed about, because of the temptations and the sins which do so easily beset me.*
>
> *And when I desire to rejoice, my heart groaneth because of my sins; nevertheless, I know in whom I have trusted. And why should I yield to sin, because of my flesh? Yea, why should I give way to temptations, that the evil one have place in my heart to destroy my peace and afflict my soul? Why am I angry because of mine enemy? O Lord, wilt thou redeem my soul? Wilt thou deliver me out of the hands of mine enemies? Wilt thou make me that I may shake at the appearance of sin? O Lord, wilt thou encircle me around in the robe of thy righteousness! O Lord, wilt thou make a way for mine escape before mine enemies! Wilt thou make my path straight before me! Wilt thou not place a stumbling block in my way—but that thou wouldst clear my way before me, and hedge not up my way, but the ways of mine enemy.* [2 Nephi 4:17-19,27,31,33]

Do we "shake at the appearance of sin" in our lives? Does our soul grieve because of our iniquities? Nephi, the righteous prophet that he was, was certainly not grieving because of any serious sin, but of the little ones that "so easily beset" him. But yet his concern was great and his desire strong to overcome them.

Nephi was talking about freeing himself from the little and petty sins of daily life. What are the "sins which do so easily beset" us? Each person's list will be different. Perhaps they may include the sins of unkindness, harshness, rudeness, unvirtuous thought, ingratitude, thoughtlessness, pride, arrogance, insensitivity to the feelings and needs of others, lightmindedness, unrighteous dominion, irreverence, gossip, bitterness, jealousy, hurt feelings or resentment. The list is certainly not all-inclusive, but mainly illustrative. We should be seriously striving to overcome these "sins". Nephi was not content to be less righteous than was possible. His standard was Jesus Christ, nothing less. He was striving for perfection. If we would have charity, we, too, must be earnestly striving for perfection in this life.

CHAPTER EIGHT

CONCLUSION

Charity, the pure love of Christ, can be a divine motivational force in our lives. It is one of the essential qualities of eternal life or God's life. Encompassed within charity is the divine power of God and divine happiness. To experience charity is to experience such power and joy.

Charity is a gift of God available to us in mortality upon certain divine conditions. The Savior and Heavenly Father eagerly await to give us this gift if we will but ask and seek for it. Charity will motivate us and create in us an overwhelming desire to keep the commandments and serve others whatever the obstacles or cost.

Charity is what we should earnestly desire and seek if we would secure for ourselves and others the goal of eternal life and celestial glory. Charity is the key to gospel motivation by which we can obtain the gift of eternal life and exaltation.